THEOLOGY OF ADMINISTRATION

a biblical basis
for organizing the
congregation

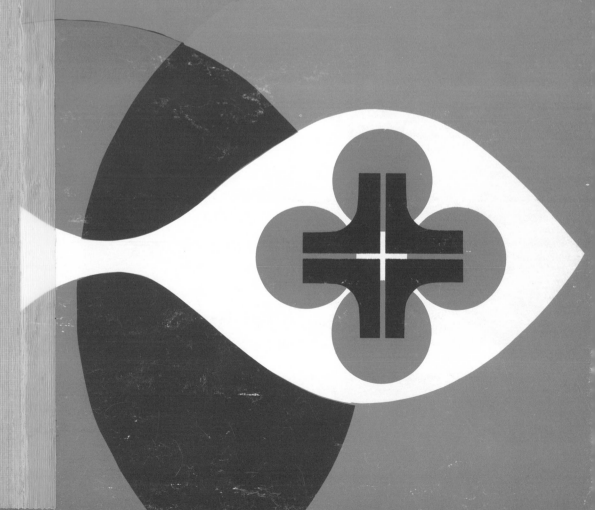

Contents

Foreword

The Rev. Harris Lee speaks from twin vantage points—twenty years in parish pastoral service and Doctor of Ministry studies. He asks that church administration be accountable to church theology. In a brief but cogent way, readers with an interest in administration are assisted in relating secular tools and disciplines to the ministry and mission of the people of God within the church.

There are available many excellent publications devoted to administration in the church or to a theology of the church. Several are listed in the bibliography and referred to in the text. But this booklet differs in that it seeks to relate both disciplines to one another. Pastor Lee sees administration and theology as contextually supportive and consistent, reflecting a church that is undivided and whole—human and divine, secular and sacred, present minded and future minded.

Pastor Lee meets a pressing need for readers seeking to blend administration and theology in the life and mission of the Christian congregation.

John Dewey

Preface

Church people have different attitudes toward administration. Some pastors speak scornfully of it, resent it, and regard it as a necessary evil. Others attend workshops and read books on the subject, experiment with new administrative ideas and techniques, thinking it is the cure for whatever ails the church and the key to its renewal.

When pastors express frustration with the amount of their administrative work, church members are usually quick to sympathize. But when the pastor neglects administrative work and the result is chaos, they are quick to murmur what a "poor organizer" the pastor is. Pastors, in turn, adamantly insist that they are to preach, teach, and administer the sacraments—not "run the whole church."

Is there a way to resolve this dilemma? Can administration be seen as a legitimate, as well as necessary, expression of ministry? Can our administrative practices be in harmony with our theological convictions? In the pages that follow we will engage such questions.

1. Administration in the Church

What do we mean by *administration?* Some distinguish *administration* from *management*. Others use these two words interchangeably. In the context of church life, administration may be defined as a discipline helping the church to order its life, enabling it to move toward the fulfillment of its mission. When defined in this way, administration touches everything a congregation does that contributes to the fulfillment of its mission.

The Word and sacraments are "administered." Administration concerns itself with the spiritual care and nurture of the congregation, its faith development, and its witness to the community. Indeed, administration ought to be seen as a gift of the Spirit that serves the common good of the church (see 1 Cor. 12:28).

Seen more narrowly, administration is concerned with specific functions: *leading, planning, organizing, staffing,* and *coordinating.*

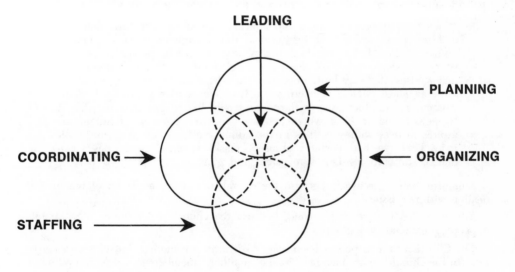

Leading is the most inclusive of the functions because it overlaps the others. It is the art of influencing people to work for the achievement of individual or group goals.

Planning involves determining a course of action for the future. It includes assessment of needs; setting of goals, priorities, and procedures; and provision for review.

Organizing includes structuring of groups for life and work, clarifying relationships, assigning responsibilities, delegating authority, and establishing accountability.

Staffing encompasses selecting, training, and developing the skills of people for the work that needs to be done.

Coordinating refers to the synchronizing of a group's efforts so that they are timely and of sufficient quantity and quality.

We have defined administration. But a second question remains: *Why* administration?

Administration is necessary, *first,* because the church is people—flesh and blood human beings with strengths, weaknesses, gifts, and longings. We do not minister in an abstract, ideal community. No less than any secular organization, the church needs to do things properly and in good order.

One objection to the use of administrative theory and practice in the church is that it applies a "secular" discipline to a "spiritual" community. Dare we employ a secular discipline within the church? While such concern for integrity is appropriate, and while we affirm that the church is God's arena, it should be remembered that the church is also human.

Scripture indicates that while the church began and is sustained by God's call, it also began and is sustained by human response. Without the initiative and call of God there would be no church, but neither would there be a church apart from human response.

The church never is enhanced by denying its humanness, or its similarities to other human organizations. The church is not to be "of the world," for it is of God and is sustained and empowered by his Word and Spirit. But the church is still "in the world" —a community of human beings, historical and finite—subject to the same forces and influences that affect other human communities.

Furthermore, as James Dittes points out, it is because the church is stubbornly human that administrative encounters often become the occasion for ministry:

> When the purposes of church and ministry, the knotty structural demands and trivial annoyances of institutions, the ambiguous purposes, limited visions, earnest but feeble faithfulness, and downright perversity of minister and people—when all these get tangled up together into minor and major crises, this may be the occasion that demands the most creative and virile of ministry. Here is where a real issue confronts real people. Perhaps it is not as grand an issue as those one would like to preach about, but it happens to be an issue where people—who are seldom as grand as one aspires to deal with—are. It is in the administrative snarls that one is far more likely to find passions aroused, masks lowered, neat roles abandoned, stubborn resistances revealed, and glimmering aspirations bared.[1]

Administration is necessary because the church is human, made up of real people dealing with real issues.

Administration is necessary, *second,* because the church is corporate, a community of people functioning as a group.

The Christian faith is personal—no one can believe for another—but it is also corporate. In the church we are members "one of another," members of God's family, mem-

---

1. James E. Dittes, *Minister on the Spot* (New York: Pilgrim Press, 1972), p. 118.

bers of Christ's body. The administrative functions mentioned earlier—leading, planning, organizing, staffing, and coordinating—are essential in the church because the church is a corporate body with a corporate life and mission.

The Scriptures use a variety of images to convey this corporate reality. In addition to *body of Christ* and *family of God* are such images as *household of God, people of God, holy nation,* and *royal priesthood.* The New Testament never is concerned with merely bringing people to faith (even if faith in Jesus Christ). Its broader concern is that they be incorporated into the body of believers.

Without administration the church is like an orchestra warming up before a concert. There is much noise and movement, but no unity or direction. Worst of all, there is no music. The task of administration in the church is analogous to that of the conductor of an orchestra: to enable collected individuals to function as a unit.

When two or more people agree to do something together, administration is necessary. The purposes of the group effort need to be understood, goals clarified, and resources identified, summoned, and deployed. All this is the work of administration, necessary because the church is corporate.

Administration in the church is necessary, *third,* because the church has a mission. Without careful planning and execution, that mission never can be carried out. The church's mission can be described in various ways: preaching the gospel; making disciples of all nations; increasing love for God and neighbor.

Here is a four-part description of the church's mission. Each part describes a result in the lives of people:

First, the church's mission is to lead people on a spiritual journey, fostering, nourishing, and developing their faith in Christ, enabling them to know the abundant life he promised. *Second,* the church's mission is to foster, nourish, and develop a sense of community among believers, providing for supportive relationships and resulting in the awareness of being loved and cared for. *Third,* the church's mission is to reach out to others with the invitation to embark on the journey of faith and join the community of faith. *Fourth,* the church's mission is to go into the world, both corporately and through its individual members, working to enable people to live governed by love, justice, righteousness, and freedom.

If the church is to fulfill its mission, many things will be required: the presence and power of the Holy Spirit, faithful preaching and teaching, fervent prayer, and committed people. But unless there is appropriate leadership, planning, organizing, staffing, and coordinating, there can be little movement toward the fulfillment of the church's mission. To say it in another way, unless there is effective administration, the church's resources may be largely wasted and the church's mission will flounder. Administration is necessary because the church has a mission.

Administration is not peripheral to the life and work of the church. It is actually inherent in the church's nature and mission. It is necessary because the church is people—corporate people with a mission.

2. Theology for Church Administration

Christianity is the most materialistic of all religions. Christians confess that "the Word became flesh and dwelt among us." We believe that God uses material means to come near and bless us—the water of Baptism and the bread and wine of Holy Communion. His word continues to be expressed through the written and spoken words of living (earthly) human beings.

It is not surprising, then, that the Christian church uses resources from the secular world to carry out its mission. In his letters the Apostle Paul borrowed from philosophical categories to clarify the faith (a practice that Christian scholars continue to this day). The church uses insights from psychology to strengthen its ministries of education and pastoral care. The church draws insights from the speech-communication field to improve preaching and from art and music to enhance worship. The church borrows with benefit from the secular world.

More recently the church has turned to another secular discipline for useful insights and methods: management science. This discipline is expressed in and through the administrative practices of the church and its leaders.

This development is not without its dangers. However eclectic the church may be, it dare not adopt secular insights and methods uncritically. Administrative practices are rooted in theory. Theory builds upon philosophical assumptions. At length there are theological implications. What we believe and what we do must be congruent. Methods must be compatible with convictions. The need of a *theology* for administration is clear.

There are obstacles, however, that hinder establishing a theology for administration. One such obstacle is the disinclination to see any necessary connection between administration and theology. Administration, for some, belongs in the same category with floor buffing or coffee making. Must we encumber ourselves with theology for such activities? Why not just *do* them!

A more formidable obstacle is the fact that theology for administration does not readily suggest itself in Scripture as does, for example, a theology of creation. The Scriptures may provide illustrations of administrative practice, but they do not deal with it directly. As we shall see, a theology for administration is at best inferred from what Scripture says about a variety of things. It is not the result of direct and clear biblical teachings.

1. Administration is practiced by God's people.

Consider Moses. Despite the directive from God to lead his people to the promised land, and despite the resources that were provided, little progress was being made.

One day Moses' father-in-law, Jethro, observed the long lines of people waiting to see Moses about trivial matters, leaving him with neither time nor energy for larger concerns. Jethro advised Moses to get himself organized:

> You shall represent the people before God, and bring their cases to God; and you shall teach them the statutes and the decisions, and make them know the way in which they must walk and what they must do. Moreover choose able men . . . and place such men over the people as rulers of thousands, of hundreds, of fifties, and of tens. And let them judge the people at all times. . . . If you do this, and God so commands you, then you will be able to endure, and all this people also will go to their place in peace (Exod. 18:19-23).

Moses then used a commonplace administrative technique—delegation.

Or, consider this incident from the ministry of Jesus. Luke reports that Jesus selected workers for a special journey—one that called for a definite commitment. "No one who puts his hand to the plow and looks back is fit for the kingdom of God." It was clearly an urgent journey: "Leave the dead to bury their own dead; but as for you, go and proclaim the kingdom of God" (Luke 9:57-62).

Jesus appointed seventy additional workers "and sent them on ahead of him, two by two, into every town and place where he himself was about to come." And he said to them, "The harvest is plentiful, but the laborers are few . . ." (Luke 10:1, 2).

The record of this journey continues for ten chapters. The casual observer may think it a long and meandering, perhaps even aimless, trek. But Luke indicates that Jesus was clear about his goal, and he repeatedly renewed his commitment to it: "He set his face to go to Jerusalem" (9:51). "He went on his way through towns and villages, teaching, and journeying toward Jerusalem" (13:22). "And taking the twelve, he said to them, 'Behold we are going up to Jerusalem, and everything that is written of the Son of man by the prophets will be accomplished'" (18:31). In spite of diversions and interruptions—natural and inherent parts of the journey—the goal was clear throughout. Jesus practiced *goal setting*, a common administrative technique.

Next, consider the Apostle Paul as he sought to raise money for the Jerusalem church (2 Cor. 8–9). Paul assumed the role of *leader*, exercising initiative and providing direction and motivation. It is evident, too, that Paul *planned* the whole effort with foresight and care, sending Titus at the appropriate time with a letter from Paul himself. Paul arranged the appeal to be well *organized* and *coordinated*. Paul was a preacher-teacher-evangelist, but he also exercised *oversight* in the church and between congregations. His use of administrative skills is evident.

2. Administration is God's gift to the church.

"God has appointed in the church first apostles, second prophets, third teachers, then workers of miracles, then healers, helpers, administrators, speakers in various kinds of tongues" (1 Cor. 12:28).

The Greek word for administrator is *kubernesis*. It is used to describe the role of a helmsman on a ship. *The Theological Dictionary of the New Testament* provides a helpful paragraph that relates *kubernesis* to other gifts mentioned in the Corinthians passage.

> The reference can only be to the specific gifts which qualify a Christian to be a helmsman to his congregation, i.e., a true director of its order and therewith of its life. What was the scope of this directive activity in the time of Paul we do not know. This was a period of fluid development. The importance of the helmsman increases in a time of storm. The office of directing the congregation may well have developed especially in emer-

gencies both within and without. The proclamation of the Word was not originally this. . . . No society can exist without some order and direction. It is the grace of God to give gifts which equip for government. The striking point is that when in verse 29 Paul asks whether all are apostles, whether all are prophets, or whether all have gifts of healing, there are no corresponding questions in respect to *antilenpseis* and *kubernesis*. There is a natural reason for this. If necessary, any member of the congregation may step in to serve as *deacon* or *ruler*. Hence these offices, as distinct from those mentioned in verse 29, may be elective. But this does not alter the fact that for their proper discharge the charisma of God is indispensable.[1]

What conclusions should be drawn from this? Clearly this: administration is neither a necessary evil nor merely a set of techniques. Administration is, rather, an entirely legitimate form of ministry, inherent to the church's life, given as a gift from God.

The theory and practice of administration for use in the church is drawn more from the secular world, however, than from Scripture or theology. St. Paul calls administrative ability a gift of God, but Scripture does not indicate *how* to administer, what *techniques* to use or refrain from using, nor does it spell out any philosophy or *theory* of administrative practice. Theology for administration must, therefore, be derived from other beliefs and teachings of the church.

Before examining some of the beliefs and teachings that influence administrative practice, it may be useful to describe several different stances that one can take. Because administration is a secular discipline, it may be helpful here to review a study by H. Richard Niebuhr. In *Christ and Culture* he outlines various ways the church has related to the secular culture.[2]

1. **Christ against culture.** Some Christians try to reject the insights and learnings from the secular world and, specifically, in view of the subject of this booklet, its administrative insights and learnings.

2. **Christ and culture.** The second stance identified by Niebuhr is the opposite of the first. It sees Christ and culture to be in essential agreement. It would lead us without reservation to use learnings from the secular world, including what it says about the art and practice of administration.

3. **Christ above culture.** The third stance argues that Christ is the fulfillment of culture's aspirations and the restorer of its institutions. This stance does not view the secular world uncritically, but neither does it reject the world. When applied to administration in the church, this stance would suggest we add to and reshape any administrative techniques that are already useful and good.

4. **Christ and culture in paradox.** Culture makes legitimate claims upon us, says this view, but so does Christ. The two claims are often in tension, sometimes in conflict, and whoever adopts this stance lives in two worlds. For administrative practice, this approach would encourage us to be faithful to Christ in our personal lives and to apply secular techniques to the institutional church.

5. **Christ transforming culture.** This is the "conversionist" position. Culture is neither accepted nor rejected. It is rather the scene of Christ's transforming influence. When adapted for church administration, this view alters the administrative methods and techniques found in the secular world, converting them for appropriate use in the church.

Because each of these five stances has been affirmed and practiced by some Christians (often with a carefully articulated rationale or theology), it can be assumed that

1. Gerhard Kittel and Gerhard Friedrich, eds., *Theological Dictionary of the New Testament* (Grand Rapids: Wm. B. Eerdmans Publishing Co.), p. 1036.
2. H. Richard Niebuhr, *Christ and Culture* (New York: Harper and Row, 1951).

there is truth in each of them. However, a combination of the third and the fifth options is proposed. The third sees Christ *above* culture, reshaping culture's administrative practices. The fifth sees Christ *transforming* culture, anticipating that administrative theory and methods from the secular world can be used beneficially in the church. Seeing Christ as the transformer of culture, the church administrator will make selective use of secular insights, altering them as necessary.

With this as the general framework, let us look now at some key teachings of the church. They can suggest implications for administration and illustrate how practices from the secular world may be transformed.

God the Father. The Nicene Creed reminds us that God is "the Father, the Almighty, maker of heaven and earth, of all that is, seen and unseen." The world is *one*. We may speak of a secular world, as distinguished from the world of the church, but there is in fact only one world, and God is creator and Lord of all.

This awareness has a freeing effect upon the Christian, and not least of all upon those called to administer the church. The secular world, too, is God's. The doctrine of creation gives us permission to look to the secular world for resources that can help the church carry out its work as an agent of redemption.

The doctrine of the incarnation. "The Word became flesh and dwelt among us." We are thus assured that God affirms the whole world, the secular as well as the religious. Indeed, as the Nicene Creed expresses it, "through him all things were made." The Creed goes on to explain, however, that the incarnation was primarily for another purpose—"for us and for our salvation." The church administrator will view the administrative techniques and practices of the secular world with that in mind. He or she will not simply adopt what is available in the surrounding culture, applying it in whatever way possible and according to "what seems to work best." The intent, rather, will be to transform or adapt what is available for use in the church.

The authors of *Ten Faces of Ministry* speak of a "gospel-informed and gospel-shaped" administration, and also of a "gospel-tinged" administration.[3] They direct a series of questions toward leaders of congregations who seek to exercise their responsibilities in light of the gospel:

> What does this (administrative practice) do to people within our congregation? Does it open up to them greater opportunities for freedom and responsibility in the gospel? Does it give them greater opportunity for being part of God's people? . . . Does our administrative style offer members opportunity to take responsibility commensurate with their gifts? [4]

The doctrine of the incarnation would affirm our use of secular administrative techniques while alerting us to the necessity, sometimes, of transforming them. Our goal is that administrative practices in the church become "gospel-tinged."

The doctrine of the Holy Spirit. "We believe in the Holy Spirit, the Lord, the giver of life, who proceeds from the Father and the Son." This doctrine teaches us that God is present to guide and empower us for living in his kingdom. Richard Hutcheson refers to the Holy Spirit as the church's organizational key—"the wheel within the wheel"—that sustains the work of the church.[5]

Some Christians assume that our belief in the Holy Spirit ought to produce a church structure and an administrative style that is loose and flexible, for the Spirit moves

3. Milo L. Brekke, Merton P. Strommen, and Dorothy L. Williams, *Ten Faces of Ministry: Perspectives on Pastoral Effectiveness Based on Survey of 5000 Lutherans* (Minneapolis: Augsburg Publishing House, 1979), p. 146.

4. Ibid.

5. Richard G. Hutcheson Jr., *Wheel Within the Wheel* (Atlanta: John Knox Press, 1979), p. 162.

"where it wills" (John 3:8). Then, it is argued, the Spirit can move within and among us, affording people the freedom to respond.

Stephen Mott argues persuasively, however, "that we are obligated by biblical examples and teaching to apply reason and order to the powers given by the Spirit of God." [6] He points to the early church, which took both the Holy Spirit and church order seriously. Both were seen as complementary. It was understood that if the church lives spiritually, it also will live orderly. Because the spiritual realm may be occupied by spirits other than the Spirit of God, says Mott, rational consideration and order must be applied.[7]

For the church administrator, the doctrine of the Holy Spirit suggests, on the one hand, that administrative techniques should be used in the church. The Spirit is present to guide and empower, and can work through methods. On the other hand, because the Spirit is of God (and therefore transcendent), he may work independently of our administrative practices and, at times, confound them.

The priesthood of all believers. Unfortunately, the priesthood of all believers is often understood to mean that every Christian is his or her own priest. Such an individualistic interpretation is inadequate. This doctrine means more—that everyone is a priest to everyone else in the Christian community. Christians are to offer themselves to one another and to pray for one another so that the work of Christ can more effectively be done. Moreover, this work is to be done not only—nor even primarily—in the church. It is to be done outside the church building, in the world of everyday affairs.

The life of a congregation should be structured and programmed so that the members are equipped to be priests in their daily lives. While this doctrine may well encourage lay people to read the Scripture, lead in prayer, and distribute the bread and wine at worship, such activities are peripheral to the central meaning of the doctrine. Administration that is theologically sound will, in view of this doctrine, work to turn the church toward the world for which Christ died.

> **Theology for administration can be inferred from the teachings of Scripture and drawn from key doctrines of the church. This theology, when put into practice, helps the church to be faithful to its Lord in pursuit of the life and mission he gives it.**

---

6. John E. Biersdorf, ed., *Creating an Intentional Ministry* (Nashville: Abingdon Press, 1976), p. 220.
7. Ibid., p. 231.

3. Can a Servant Be a Leader?

God's people always have had leaders. Before the time of Christ, such figures as Abraham, Moses, Joshua, and Jeremiah stood out as leaders. The twelve disciples, and particularly Peter, James, and John, were leaders in the early church, as was the Apostle Paul. Jesus himself was a leader, and his "gifts" to the church—apostles, prophets, evangelists, pastors, and teachers—were in the form of leaders. The purpose was "to equip the saints for the work of ministry, for building up the body of Christ" (Eph. 4:11, 12).

The need for leaders in the church continues. The Letter of Pastoral Call currently in use in two major American denominations affirms the leadership role of the pastor: "[This] church recognizes the office of pastor, established by our Lord, and seeks through it to give the pastoral leadership and care necessary for the establishment and nurture of Christ's church." In addition, education directors, musicians, parish workers, business administrators, youth workers, secretaries, and various other associates are often employed by congregations to serve in leadership capacities.

Congregations also elect or appoint other leaders from among their membership. Teachers; members of boards, committees, and task forces; liturgical assistants; and church council members all assume leadership roles.

In Chapter 1, it was noted that leadership is the most inclusive of administrative functions, overlapping planning, organizing, staffing, and coordinating, as well as finding expression through each of them. Because leadership is so inclusive, it becomes a complex task. Therefore, it may be helpful to examine the nature of leadership and the variety of styles it might emulate.

On one level, the role of the leader is easy to describe. In wagon-train language, "A leader is someone who knows how to get you to high ground and good water by camp time." That description, while an obvious oversimplification, has within it a central truth. The leader must have a goal clearly in mind and be able to bring the group to it in the appropriate time.

How to determine goals will be discussed in Chapter 7. But first, consider the role of the leader as he or she seeks to influence individuals and groups to follow and to move toward the fulfillment of some goal.

THE HUMAN SCIENCES

Before turning to Scripture for insights on leadership let us turn to the human sciences. These disciplines can help us understand more fully the dynamics of leadership.

13

The human sciences describe two general dimensions of leadership: *tasks* and *individuals*. The following diagram is adapted from one by Robert Blake and Jane Mouton.[1]

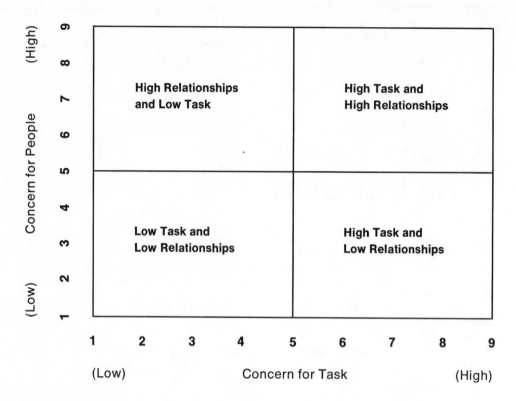

Concern for *task* is illustrated on the horizontal axis. A leader with a rating of 9 on this line has a maximum concern for the task. What counts, according to such a leader, is "getting the job done."

Concern for *relationships* is illustrated on the vertical axis. As a leader's rating climbs on this scale, it reveals an increasing concern for relationships. To a leader with a rating of 9, what counts is good morale and happy relationships.

Church leaders are appropriately concerned about both tasks and relationships. The church cannot focus entirely on the relationships of its members, for it has a task to accomplish beyond itself. But neither can it focus on task to the neglect of relationships. Church leaders must be concerned about both. The ideal orientation is a 9-9 on the diagram (the upper right hand corner).

The human sciences also help to identify leadership styles. These range from *authoritarian* to *laissez-faire*. Between these extremes are various degrees of participatory democracy. Authoritarian leaders make frequent appeals to positions when exercising their role. They may consult with others on their team and, at times, may work for a consensus, but few votes are taken. Authoritarian leaders make most of the decisions and announce them when necessary or appropriate.

The laissez-faire style provides virtually no leadership at all. Such leaders give mini-

1. Robert R. Blake and Jane S. Mouton, *The Managerial Grid* (Houston: Gulf Publishing Co., 1964), p. 99.

mum direction and provide maximum freedom for group decision, taking a nondirective approach to decision making and administration.

Between the two extremes, and covering a wider spectrum, is the democratic style, sometimes called *participatory democracy*. The diagram below is adapted from one by Robert Tannebaum and Warren Schmidt.[2] It illustrates a leadership style continuum, ranging from authoritarian (far left) to laissez-faire (far right). There are various degrees of participatory democracy in between.

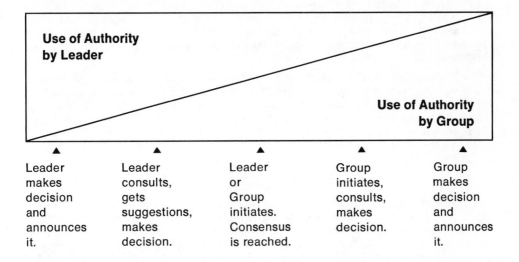

| Leader makes decision and announces it. | Leader consults, gets suggestions, makes decision. | Leader or Group initiates. Consensus is reached. | Group initiates, consults, makes decision. | Group makes decision and announces it. |

The participatory democratic style is used by those who believe the best way to motivate others is to involve them in decision making. This results in a greater sense of group ownership and a willingness to support decisions once they have been made.

Is there a *best* style? Research indicates that the notion of a single, best style is unsound. Leadership is a function that involves so many variables that a single style is impractical and ineffective. Effective leaders, in the church as well as in secular organizations, adapt their style in response to specific situations.

While there is no style that will serve best under all circumstances, it should be noted that those who affirm the "systems approach" to organizational life (see Chapter 6) favor participatory democracy. This style takes a holistic view and is aware that the life of an organization is influenced by environment. Moreover, this style seems especially appropriate in the church, for it gives expression to the church's convictions about the priesthood of all believers.

In addition to these two dimensions and three styles of leadership, the human sciences identify two distinct leadership *types*.

James MacGregor Burns calls these two types "transactional" and "transforming."[3]

Transactional leadership. The focus is more on *means* than on ends, though the ends need not be subdued or ignored. The transactional leader develops a cooperative interchange with his or her followers, with the aim of exchanging one thing for another—jobs for votes, perhaps, or goods for services. Transactional leaders do not necessarily

2. Robert Tannebaum and Warren Schmidt, "How to Choose a Leadership Pattern," *Harvard Business Review* (March-April 1957), p. 99.
3. James MacGregor Burns, *Leadership* (New York: Harper and Row, 1979).

serve to enable a joint effort of a group toward a common good. They may at times achieve that end, but the focus is on means, not ends. This type of leadership may simply encourage persons or groups with individual interests to go (or continue going) their separate ways.

Transforming leadership. Attention is given to the end result. While less concerned about the means of achieving an end than is transactional leadership, transforming leadership does emphasize and exercise one primary means: teaching. With the aid of teaching it intends to change (transform) participants so that they are united in a common goal or course. "The premise of this leadership," says Burns, "is that, whatever the separate interests persons might hold, they are presently or potentially united in the pursuit of higher goals, the realization of which is tested by the achievement of significant change that represent the collective or pooled interests of leaders and followers." [4]

The *transactional* leader taps the felt or expressed needs of the participants. The *transforming* leader, while perhaps using the needs of the participants as a point of contact, seeks to raise their aspirations, shape their values, and mobilize their potential. The secret of transforming leadership, says Burns, is "that people can be lifted into their better selves." [5]

SCRIPTURE

The priestly role. This leader is a mediator between God and man. In the Old Testament era, priests offered sacrifices on behalf of the people and conveyed God's blessings to the people. Israel as a whole had priestly functions among the nations, functions specified in Isaiah 61: to bind the broken, liberate the captives, release the imprisoned, and comfort those who mourn. Jesus assumed the priestly role at the beginning of his public ministry when he quoted and applied to himself the Isaiah passage: "The Spirit of the Lord is upon me, because he has anointed me to preach good news to the poor. He has sent me to proclaim release to the captives and recovering of sight to the blind, to set at liberty those who are oppressed, to proclaim the acceptable year of the Lord" (Luke 4:18-19).

In the priestly role, church leaders will be pastoral toward those whom they are called to lead, sensitive to their needs and interests, reflecting a personal and caring approach. Like transactional leadership, it focuses on means rather than ends, on the interests and needs of individuals, sometimes to the neglect of the group.

The prophetic role. The prophet is also a mediator, but the primary direction is from God to man. The prophets were God's voices, declaring God's will and way, calling for justice and righteousness, reminding the people of their mission. Even as he assumed a priestly role, Jesus often took upon himself the role of a prophet, speaking the corrective word, declaring God's will and purpose, urging the people to change their lives accordingly.

The prophetic role has a certain affinity to transforming leadership. It is leadership that seeks to bring about change in the lives of the followers and in the life of the group; transforming and prophetic leadership seeks to unite people in the pursuit of higher goals, whether understood as moral values or as the will of God.

Can the priestly and prophetic roles be held together? Can a church leader hold the two in healthy tension? It appears that this is what Jesus did. It appears also that leaders in the church should strive to do the same.

---

4. Ibid., pp. 425-426.
5. Ibid., p. 462.

For the church leader there is therefore:

a time to work for stability and a time to work for change;

a time to establish goals according to the needs of people and a time to establish goals according to the will of God;

a time to build up the fellowship and a time to engage in mission;

a time to accept people where they are and a time to urge them to become what they can be;

a time to be priestly or transactional and a time to be prophetic or transforming.

Church leaders dare not assume either prophetic or priestly roles to the exclusion of the other. They need to embrace them both. Priestly and prophetic functions need to coexist creatively, simultaneously, within the same leader.

It is a difficult task, for it requires a balancing of opposites. The ministry of our Lord provides the church leader with a model that brings about at least a partial synthesis of the two opposites.

The servant role. Jesus took upon himself the separate roles of priest and prophet. The prominent image of Christ in the Gospels, however, is that of a servant. Jesus used creatively the servant role to synthesize the roles of prophet and priest. Those roles undoubtedly shaped his servanthood—giving attention to the needs of people on the one hand and honoring the word and will of God on the other.

The servant role also holds together two leadership concerns—tasks and relationships. In addition, the servant image guides leaders in their use of authority, and in the choice of a style according to the particular circumstances. Servanthood reminds leaders that there are times when the transactional role is best.

Church leaders appropriately shy away from self-glorification and self-aggrandizement. They serve both God and people, sensitive to the needs of persons and faithful to God's word. The faithful style is that of a servant.

The effective church leader leads by serving and serves by leading.

4. Can a Leader
Be a Friend?

What makes for a thriving church? What kinds of congregations are effective in out-reach, above average in attendance at worship, and experiencing numerical growth? In upstate New York, church leaders sought answers to such questions. With the use of surveys and conversations they made some interesting—even surprising—discoveries.

Is community-oriented programming a factor? No.

Is an active evangelism committee an important factor? No. It may even be counter-productive.

Is the pastoral leadership style a factor? Yes. The style is best described as "benign authoritarian."

Is the quality of the worship life a factor? Yes. No congregation from among those considered grew unless its worship was positive and uplifting.

The key factor in congregational growth and vitality was found elsewhere, however. It concerned how well the people nurture and support one another, how well they help others feel loved, cared for, and wanted. Congregations that provided for the nurture of significant relationships were effective in reaching others, had above average attendance at worship, and were growing in numbers.[1]

These research findings point to the horizontal dimension of the church's life, and to the importance of good relationships among members of a congregation. Scripture has long referred to church members as sisters and brothers in the faith, as members of God's family. Church people are asking that a sense of this family or community be made evident. They want to know the other members as friends.

Jurgen Moltmann emphasizes the friendship factor in the church by pointing out that it is rooted in our relationship with God. "In the fellowship of Jesus the disciples become friends of God. In the fellowship of Jesus they no longer experience God as Lord, nor only as Father; rather they experience him in his innermost nature as Friend." [2]

This awareness, says Moltmann, leads to an "open friendship" between and among the members of the church. We are no more and no less than a "fellowship of the friends of Jesus." He writes:

---

1. *Action Information*, vol. 3, no. 3 (Alban Institute, Inc., Sept. 1977), pp. 4-6.
2. Jürgen Moltmann, *The Passion for Life: A Messianic Lifestyle*, tr. and intro. M. Douglas Meeks (Philadelphia: Fortress Press, 1978), p. 57.

Friendship is an unpretentious relationship, for "friend" is not an official term, nor a title of honor, nor a function. It is a personal designation. Friendship unites affection with respect. There is no need to bow to a friend. We can look him in the eye. We neither look up to him nor down on him. In friendship we experience ourselves for what we are, respected and accepted in our own freedom. Through friendship we respect and accept other people as people and as individual personalities. Friendship combines affection with loyalty. One can rely on a friend.[3]

This raises questions for the leaders of congregations. What can leaders do to strengthen the quality of friendship within the congregation? Can church leaders be friends to those whom they lead?

Dietrich Bonhoeffer observed that there are seeds of discord in every Christian community—a fact that the community does well to face squarely at the outset. He went on to speak of several "ministries" that would help prevent the seeds of discord from taking root:

The ministry of holding one's tongue. In contrast to popular counsel inviting people to be "open and honest" about their thoughts and feelings towards one another, Bonhoeffer stressed that "it must be a decisive rule of every Christian fellowship that each individual is prohibited from saying much that occurs to him." [4] This, said Bonhoeffer, will put to rest the scrutinizing, judging, condemning attitudes that so easily become prevalent in the Christian community.

The ministry of listening. Listening is a basic expression of love, said Bonhoeffer. We need to listen to one another. As our failure to listen to the Word of God leads to the death of the spiritual life, so our failure to listen to others leads to the death of our relationships with them. A friend listens.

The ministry of bearing one another's burdens. The Apostle Paul said that bearing one another's burdens is one way of fulfilling the law of Christ. According to Bonhoeffer such burdens include the burden of forgiveness. When a brother or sister has disrupted the fellowship, harmony can be restored only through forgiveness.

The ministries that Bonhoeffer described should be performed by all members of the church, including those with leadership responsibilities. Indeed, leaders are called to lead here, too—to be examples for others in the ministries of holding one's tongue, of listening, of bearing one another's burdens. These are ministries that build and strengthen friendships.

What should be the *attitude* of church leaders towards those whom they lead? It can be described in various ways: an attitude of positive regard; of supportiveness; of genuine caring. The leader's attitude is to be one of concern for the welfare of the people in the congregation—an attitude that says, in effect, "I care about your well-being; I want the best for you; I want to deal with you with integrity."

This attitude must be balanced by another. A true friend will have high expectations for others and will urge them to live up to these expectations. Leaders who fail here will soon be seen as sentimentalists by those they seek to lead. In time they will lose respect. "Nothing can be more cruel than the tenderness that consigns another to his sin," wrote Bonhoeffer. "Nothing can be more compassionate than the severe rebuke that calls a brother back from the path of sin." [5] The church leader's positive regard and genuine concern is expressed not only through warm and accepting camaraderie. It is expressed as well through the sometimes stern call to live up to expectations and possibilities.

---

3. Jürgen Moltmann, *The Church in the Power of the Spirit* (New York: Harper and Row, 1977), p. 115.
4. Dietrich Bonhoeffer, *Life Together* (New York: Harper and Row, 1954), p. 92.
5. Ibid., p. 107.

The leader's friendship is also expressed through what can be called, simply, competency in the leadership role. Some leaders try to "get by" on charm. Others depend on warmth and friendliness toward the followers. Sooner or later these are seen for what they really are—subtle forms of manipulation and, ultimately, unfriendly and unloving kinds of leadership.

Andrew Greeley describes several leadership functions, the competent use of which makes possible gracious relationships.[6]

He cites first what he calls *symbolic leadership*—a quality of leadership that makes the leaders "transparent" to the values and goals of the organization. There must be evidence that the leader "really believes" what he or she says, that there is a clear, enthusiastic, and articulate commitment to the goals of the organization.

> The symbolic leader plays both a prophetic and therapeutic role, which is to say, he both challenges and comforts. He stirs his followers out of their lethargy, complacency, and self-satisfaction. He is not satisfied with the way things are and he demands of those associated with him that they use the best of their talents. . . . He is also able to comfort, to reassure, to strengthen, to support. If he says to his followers that certain things must be done, he also says they are capable of doing them. His prophecy is never such as to make his associates feel inadequate. Quite the contrary, his prophecy is designed to make them feel more adequate than they were before they heard the prophecy.[7]

Greeley's second type is *ideological leadership*. Such a leader is able to see the big picture and continually remind the others of that larger picture. People tend to turn in upon themselves. The leader will often fulfill the ideological function and then serve the well-being of the organization, says Greeley, not by providing solutions or answers but by posing problems and raising questions.[8]

Third on Greeley's list is *interpersonal leadership*. The leader creates an atmosphere that provides for the development and expression of individual gifts. Interpersonal leadership also is concerned with creating an atmosphere of harmony within the group. Conflict and tension cannot always be avoided, but the effects can be minimized through proper conflict management.[9] In fact, the conflicts themselves can be minimized, or at least reduced in number, through appropriate use of personnel management skills.

The fourth and last that Greeley names is *organizational leadership*. There is no way to avoid the fact that groups of people can function only when there is organizational effort. A leadership function is therefore administrative. Someone has to preside over the implementation of the decisions made by the organization and over its life in general. The leader will either do it or see that it gets done. Greeley writes, "The leader must see to the bookkeeping and housekeeping details. It is an onerous and perhaps thankless task, and his colleagues may grumble and complain about the need to be concerned over such details. Nevertheless, they would grumble and complain much louder if the leader failed to manage for the bookkeeping and housekeeping in such a way that the organizational climate of the group did not provide some stability and order." [10]

These leadership functions call for leadership skills on the part of those who lead. Not everyone has them by nature, but all can improve their skills in each of the func-

6. Andrew M. Greeley, *Unsecular Man* (New York: Dell Publishing Co., 1974), pp. 232-239.
7. Ibid., pp. 232-233.
8. Ibid., p. 233.
9. Ibid.
10. Ibid., p. 236.

tion areas. This can lead to more effective expression of leadership and, in turn, to a more effective community. It is an important way for leaders to express their friendship and their genuine concern for those whom they lead.

Can a leader be a friend? Yes! But such friendship is of a particular quality. It is a friendship that provides for positive relationships, yet recognizes and honors other realities of organizational life.

While we are rightly concerned about shared leadership, about collegiality and friendship, we also must face the fact that leaders are given responsibility—and accompanying authority. As in all organizations, within the church some are given greater responsibility than others. Their calling, under God and within the community of faith, is still to fulfill their responsibility as best they can. Leaders dare not neglect their responsibility. Nor can others be allowed to usurp them—not even in the name of friendship.

Neither must leaders discount the reality and presence of sin. While it may be true that the more people live with one another as friends the less they need to be concerned about structure and organization, it is also true that our ability to live together as friends is conditioned by sin's brokenness. On a church staff or church council, for example, unless responsibility is designated—along with sufficient authority—the group will be dominated by the most assertive and articulate member. Unless the will-to-power is checked and balanced, the result will be either dictatorship or anarchy—but in neither case friendship.

> **A leader can be a friend, if he or she is able to be a particular kind of friend— one who stirs people out of their lethargy, complacency, and self-satisfaction when that is the need; one who stands alongside with loyalty and affection when that is the need. A friend encourages, exhorts, questions, and demands, as well as comforts, reassures, and supports.**

5. Those Who Administer the Church

Who administers the church? The pastor? The lay chairperson? The church council? The congregation as a whole? A combination of them all? The question takes on a new urgency in light of a recent phenomenon—the rediscovery of the laity, rooted in the awareness that the ministry of the church belongs to the members themselves.

Christ's Great Commission—to go, make disciples, baptize, and teach—was given to the church as a whole (Matt. 28:19-20). When Ephesians describes Christ's gifts to the church—apostles, prophets, evangelists, pastors, and teachers—it says they were given to the church "to equip the saints for the work of ministry" (Eph. 4:11-13). The first letter of Peter refers to the church as "a chosen race, a royal priesthood, a holy nation, God's own people." The purpose, we are told, is to "declare the wonderful deeds of him who called you out of darkness into his marvelous light" (1 Peter 2:9). These passages reflect what Scripture as a whole teaches: the ministry of the church is given by God to the whole church.

But in the church, as in any organization, everybody's business quickly becomes nobody's business. While the members of the church are scattered throughout the community and world, where they serve as salt and light, the church also has an institutional life, with many characteristics and qualities identical to secular institutions.

Because it is an institution, the church has found it useful—even necessary—to delegate some of its work to particular persons and groups. It does not abdicate the work but, rather, provides for various leadership functions so that the work of the church can thrive. Hence, boards of Christian education and education directors are given certain responsibilities, which, in turn, provide for the strengthening of the congregation's education ministry. The same is true of worship, youth, and stewardship ministries. The congregation delegates particular tasks to particular people so that it may be enabled to carry out its work effectively.

This is true also for the work of administration. If the congregation as a whole attempts to do the leading, planning, organizing, staffing, and coordinating, it will either be neglected or it will end in chaos. The work of administration must be delegated and assigned to particular persons and groups for effective congregational life.

James Anderson and Ezra Jones speak of three distinguishable administrative areas of congregational life: *spiritual direction, associational leadership,* and *organizational management.*[1]

---

1. James D. Anderson and Ezra E. Jones, *The Management of Ministry* (San Francisco: Harper and Row, 1978), pp. 78-106.

Spiritual direction includes the preaching, teaching, and sacramental ministries of the church. It deals with religious education programs, the ministries of counseling, and crisis support.

Associational leadership is political in nature. It concerns itself with the general governance of the congregation—goal setting, conflict management, consensus formulation, evangelism, and social ministries.

Organizational management attends to maintaining the organization and its programs of fund raising, building maintenance, financial management, and the management of task groups. The administrative tasks of planning, leading, organizing, staffing, and coordinating—when applied to the internal life of the church—belong especially to the *organizational management* area of the administrative work.

But when all is said and done, *who* administers the church? It is tempting to say that the pastor or pastors provide the spiritual direction, and that the lay president is the chief administrator in the areas of associational leadership and organizational management. This arrangement, though perhaps assumed by a majority of church members, is unworkable for at least four reasons:

1. It assumes that the three areas are not only distinguishable but also separable.
2. It assumes that the lay leader has both the time and the ability to fulfill the responsibilities of the two administrative areas.
3. It assumes that this is what the congregation wants, both officially and practically.
4. It assumes that it represents a theologically sound division of responsibilities.

All four assumptions are flawed. **First,** while separate administrative areas can be identified, they are not finally separable. They overlap; they are interdependent; they are meant to be integrated. Preaching and teaching are meant to be "wedded" to associational leadership and organizational management.

Second, only in rare cases does the lay leader have both the time and ability to be the chief administrator in the areas of associational leadership and organizational management. Every congregation has men and women with available *time*—and willingness to give it—for the work of the church. Every congregation also has men and women with the *ability* to provide the necessary administrative leadership. But there are comparatively few volunteers in a typical congregation who have both. It would be hazardous to structure a congregation on the premise that the congregational president has both time and ability to do significant administrative work.

Third, congregations generally do not expect their lay president to serve as a chief administrative officer. Some congregations actually state such expectations in writing. In actual practice, however, it becomes clear that even in these parishes the responsibility really lies elsewhere. Where, in fact, *does* responsibility lie in most congregations? To put the question another way, Who gets blamed when things go amiss? Who picks up the pieces (or sees that they are picked up) when things fall apart? Those with much experience in ministry will agree that the answer to these questions is usually not the congregational president.

Fourth, the separation of *spiritual* leadership from *associational* and *organizational* leadership is theologically unsound, for it implies that the two latter functions are secular and to be insulated from theological influence.

Who, then, does the work of administration? First, the work of administration is a shared ministry. While it is delegated, it is delegated not to one but to several, and to both individuals and groups. This is especially true of the aspect of administration that comes under the general category of *policy making*. Here collegiality seems to be the most effective way of managing any organization, the church included.

The work of *implementing* the policies is also shared by many in a typical congregation. However, even when it is carried out by several people—volunteers and/or paid staff—it is still overseen and directed by one person.

In a few congregations—most of them small and stable—this "one person" is the lay president. He or she either carries out or directs and oversees the associated leadership and organization management areas of administrative work. More often, however, the pastor is expected to fulfill these responsibilities, in addition to those in the category of spiritual direction. Pastors may chafe under such expectations (and usually will get considerable sympathy from congregational members!) but the expectations remain. The life and well-being of the congregation depend significantly upon how effective the pastor fulfills them.

The lay president may well serve as the chief administrator in the policy-making dimension of administration. As "chairman of the board" he or she will coordinate and guide the decision-making process. But the chief administrative officer of the congregation is the pastor—or, when there is a pastoral staff with such a designation, the senior pastor. He or she will oversee and guide the implementation of the policies.

This arrangement, while opposed by some—both clergy and lay—is advocated here for several reasons:

1. *It has historic precedence.* According to *The Encyclopedia of the Lutheran Church*, administration is and has been one of the four primary functions of the ordained ministry. Along with proclaiming, teaching, and healing is the administrative function—"executive oversight of the program of the church . . ." [2]

2. *The work of administration is integral to the work of ministry as a whole.* According to the research reflected in *Ten Faces of Ministry* (a description of ministry that represents the perceptions of the majority of Lutherans in the United States)—administration is an aspect of church work necessarily assumed by ordained ministers. Along with the ministries of word and sacrament, counseling, outreach, and liturgical leadership, is the ministry of administration.

> Whether they like the idea or not, pastors cannot help administering. They may do it badly or well, but they all administer. When a conflict arises, pastors choose whether to mediate, take over and settle, or quietly escape. The choice defines the administrative style, but pastors cannot *not* administer. Money comes into and flows out of congregations. Pastors' involvement or noninvolvement with that flow of resources reveals administrative style. Points of decision arise in the church, and whether a particular decision is to buy more mimeograph paper or to take on a new staff member, the style of a pastor's involvement in that decision is administrative. People call on the phone, asking, "Who do you think ought to handle this matter?" There is no way to escape the ministry of administration. All pastors have are choices among methods of carrying it out.[3]

3. *Pastors are currently doing the work of administration.* Studies on how pastors use their time repeatedly show that a large percentage of it is given to administrative work. Results of a recent survey indicate that over one-third of all pastors questioned gave more time to administrative work than to any other function of ministry.[4] Coun-

---

2. Robert P. Roth, "Ministry," *The Encyclopedia of the Lutheran Church*, vol. 2, ed. Julius Bodensieck (Minneapolis: Augsburg Publishing House, 1965), p. 1583.
3. Brekke, Strommen, and Williams, *Ten Faces of Ministry*, pp. 144-145.
4. Charles S. Anderson, *Seminary Education Survey* (St. Paul: Luther Theological Seminary, 1973), p. 2.

seling ranked second, with one-fourth giving the most time to it. Preaching, including sermon preparation, ranked third. Approximately one out of five pastors indicated that they spend more time in that function than any other. Administrative work, for good or for ill, gets more time from more pastors than any other aspect of their work.

4. *The members of the congregation expect it.* Even congregations that officially say otherwise expect their pastors to serve as chief administrator, and hold them responsible for the well-being of the congregation, including its organizational life. As Lyle Schaller has indicated, this is especially true in large congregations:

> In the vast majority of large churches the senior pastor is expected to be and does function as the chief administrative officer of that congregation . . .

> The chief administrative officer either (a) administers the life of the large parish or (b) takes responsibility for seeing that it is done.

> The chief administrative officer makes sure there is an adequate system for the care of members and monitors the system to make sure it is working. The actual operation of that system of congregational care usually is carried out largely by others.

> The chief administrative officer monitors the whole parish system to ensure that all the components of the total ministry and program are consistent with and reinforce the basic values, roles, and goals of the congregation.

> The chief administrative officer affirms both the functional and the relationship dimensions of each staff member's work.[5]

Many pastors and lay persons object to assigning pastors a "chief administrator" role because of the negative associations it creates. "Chief administrator" projects the image of a strong-willed and perhaps overbearing boss. By contrast, "pastor" suggests a gentle and affirming shepherd. Another negative image that comes to mind for many is that of a desk-bound paper shuffler who has abdicated the role of pastor for that of bureaucratic clerk.

We can, however, find positive images for the pastor as "chief administrator."

The first of these comes from H. Richard Niebuhr—the "pastoral director." This image emerged for Niebuhr from a study of the Bible and the tradition of the church, from the needs of the present day as he perceived them, and from conversations with parish pastors.

For Niebuhr, the pastoral director image became an integrating role description, one that enabled the pastor to see the full breadth of responsibilities and work at them holistically.

Niebuhr wrote:

> In his work the pastoral director carries on all the traditional functions of the ministry—preaching, leading the worshiping community, administering the sacraments, caring for souls, presiding over the church. But as the preacher and priest organized these traditional functions in special ways so does the pastoral director. His first function is that of building or "edifying" the church; he is concerned in everything that he does to bring into being a people of God who as a church will serve the purpose of the church in the local community and the world. Preaching does not become less important for him than it was for the preacher but its aim is somewhat different. It is now pastoral preaching directed toward the instruction, the per-

---

5. Lyle E. Schaller, *The Multiple Staff and the Larger Church* (Nashville: Abingdon Press, 1980), pp. 112-114.

suasion, the counseling of persons who are becoming members of the body of Christ and who are carrying on the mission of the church.[6]

What Niebuhr says about preaching could be said about any of the pastoral tasks, including administration. All are interrelated, all are meant to be integrated, and all are directed toward the building or edifying of the church. The pastoral director image helps maintain the needed integration and direction of the various tasks.

The second positive image is that of an orchestra conductor. The authors of *Ten Faces of Ministry* offer this as a role model, and apply it especially to the pastor's responsibility for administration.[7] As the authors point out, an orchestra warming up before a concert is similar to a congregation without appropriate leadership. There is much noise and motion, but little unity or direction. The result is dissonance and discomfort for both performers and audience. The need, obviously, is for a conductor to bring order from the chaos and to give direction to the energy.

> The same kind of leadership is required of a pastor in a typical congregation, if there isn't going to be a powerful lot of chaos. Lutherans rank this area of ministry as fifth in importance, which causes it to fall into the lower "contributes very much" range of importance for effective Christian ministry. Congregations vary, of course, in their need for administrative direction; many have seemed to fare remarkably well during interims without pastoral leadership. But when this happens, the congregation may be operating on the lingering effects of past leadership, as an orchestra can continue for some time, even after the conductor steps away from the podium. But that independence is short-term. Every congregation can benefit by having a pastor who can identify the superabundance of talent, energy, and dedication present and guide it into basically harmonious joint ministry.[8]

> **The work of administration is a work shared by many in the congregation: elected leaders, staff members, volunteers, pastor. The chief administrator, however, is the pastor, who either administers the life of the church or takes responsibility for seeing that it is done.**

6. H. Richard Niebuhr, *The Purpose of the Church and Its Ministry* (New York: Harper and Row, 1956), p. 82.
7. Brekke, Strommen, and Williams, *Ten Faces of Ministry*, pp. 131-149.
8. Ibid., p. 132.

6. Organizing for Ministry

The church seeks to organize because the gifts God has given it are for its welfare and mission as a whole. Only through proper organization can these gifts be responsibly allocated. An organizational structure must be designed, policies determined, and tasks assigned if the church is to carry out its work responsibly and effectively.

In the early church good organization was a matter of considerable concern. The Apostle Paul revisited the first converts and wrote letters not only to encourage them in faith but also to instruct them on how to organize their churches. "In the early church, despite its spontaneous and charismatic character, there are definite regulations of a juridical character pertaining to marriage, support of missionaries, and treatment of grievances." [1] Paul concludes a lengthy discussion of the relationship between spiritual gifts and order by saying "all things should be done decently and in order" (1 Cor. 14:40).

The organizing work of the church is actually a mark of the seriousness with which it takes itself and its mission. Gibson Winter has written:

> One way we distinguish the commonsense world of everyday life from dreaming, fantasy, and aesthetic enjoyment is by the degree of organization expected in our activities and responses. We do not expect dreams to manifest their contents in highly organized forms. Many dreams seem to reorder haphazardly the basic theme of everyday life. Organization means a rational ordering of various elements and phases directed toward the effective realization of an anticipated state of affairs. [2]

God has revealed his nature and his mission of redemptive love. The ordering and organizing of this work is proper and necessary. God has not revealed, however, *how* we must organize the church. "Protestantism takes a pragmatic view of organization," writes Gibson Winter. "As long as agencies contribute to the preaching of the Word, the administration of the sacraments, and the maintenance of pure teaching, they are justified. In brief, Protestantism upholds a dynamic principle of order—the disclosure of the Word with power in the community of faith." [3]

The church, therefore, never has developed organizational structures that are

---

1. Biersdorf, *Creating an Intentional Ministry*, p. 221.
2. Gibson Winter, *Religious Identity: The Organization of the Major Faiths* (New York: The Macmillan Co., 1968), p. 12.
3. Ibid., p. 105.

unique to itself. It has always borrowed them from the secular environment, adapting them as deemed necessary. Yet, as Robert Worley has charged, the church has not kept current in its borrowing and adapting. "It is as though we in the church had learned nothing about organization, leadership, and maximization of human potential since Max Weber studied the Prussian Army and the Roman Catholic church and wrote a description of them that still characterizes, all too frequently, our own church organizations." [4]

What does Worley envision?

> We are working toward a contemporary biblical and theological under-
> standing of the institutional church and ministry that takes into account a
> contemporary understanding of human organizations. The aim is to bring
> about a theological understanding of the church and a theory of organi-
> zation and leadership together so that the contemporary church may be-
> come a visible expression of the faith commitments of Christians in its
> ministry and mission. [5]

Worley refers to "a theory of organization." He correctly reminds us that whatever shape an organization takes, it is rooted in theory. The theory may not be consciously held, and it may be mixed with other theories, but supporting every organizational structure and style there is theory. Peter Rudge has identified and described five different organizational theories, evaluating them for their appropriateness for the church. [6]

1. **The traditional theory** concentrates on maintaining a tradition. Although this theory has served the church reasonably well, it is seen as being too "root heavy" for a changing world and too narrow in the way it perceives the role of the church.

2. **The charismatic theory** leads to a style that can be described with the phrase "pursuing an intuition." What sometimes results is a spontaneous organization, one that is able to respond quickly to changing needs. Charismatic theory tends to lead the church away from its givens, however, and depend excessively on the vision or charisma of the leader.

3. **The classical theory** concentrates on running the organization. Its "top-down" structure usually operates smoothly and efficiently, which is one reason it is so widely used. The tendency of an organization structured according to the classical theory, however, is to focus on itself rather than on its wider mission.

4. **The human relations theory** stresses "the leading of groups." The emphasis is upon interpersonal relationships. While this theory leads to a church life that is in many ways beneficial, it tends to neglect the wholeness of the church, the interdepen-dency of the various groups, and, as in the case of the *charismatic theory*, the givens of the church.

5. **The systems theory** sees the church as a system made up of two or more sub-systems. Systems theory emphasizes relationships between the different parts of an organization, noting the influence of the parts upon each other and upon the whole. According to this theory organizations are in a continual state of adaptation to the world around them, enabling them to be both faithful and relevant to their purposes. An important liability of the systems theory is that it sounds so mechanical that some reject it without taking the time to understand it. Functionally, however, it is not mechanical, and the theory is proving itself to be valid in various kinds of organiza-tions, including the church.

---

4. Robert Worley, *Change in the Church: A Source of Hope* (Philadelphia: The Westminster Press, 1971), p. 27.
5. Ibid., p. 73.
6. Peter F. Rudge, *Ministry and Management* (London: Tavistock Publications Ltd., 1968), pp. 21-31.

Peter Rudge links the *systems theory* to the body of Christ image of the church. At the conclusion of his study he states, "the inquiry has shown that the systems way of thinking has the greatest weight of biblical support and is nearest to the central stream of Christian thinking; and so the systems theory of management is supremely suitable for use in the church." [7]

Alvin Lindgren and Norman Shawchuck come to a similar conclusion and list what they see as this theory's unique contribution to organizational theory, especially as applied to the church:

1. Systems thinking offers a perspective of wholeness, a gestalt view of the entire church that is often easily overlooked because of one's involvement in a particular organization within the church.

2. A systems view keeps the church from being totally focused in upon itself by requiring it to see itself in relationship with other systems in its environment.

3. A systems view will greatly increase the effectiveness of any planning process by identifying all the components of the church and its environment that will act as resources or constraints upon the plan.

4. The systems approach enables a leader or group to predict more accurately the effects and implications of alternative courses of action.[8]

The systems theory is advocated as most appropriate for the church. It takes seriously both the biblical givens and particular needs of the present, while honoring the wholeness of the church and interrelatedness of its various ministries. Lindgren and Shawchuck explain:

If an organization is primarily task oriented, a bureaucratic style will prove most effective. If an organization is primarily person oriented, a human-relations style will prove most effective. If, however, the organization understands persons to need organizations and structure in order to achieve its organizational goals, a systems approach will prove most effective, since systems theory holds the organizational goals and the goals of persons to be of equal importance. Systems theory addresses the interrelatedness of the organization and its people.[9]

Moreover, systems theory enables one to view the church as a living synthesis—even an organic one (as St. Paul describes it with his image "body of Christ"). It means that no individual group, committee, or ministry is autonomous, independent, or isolated from other boards, agencies, and operations of the parish. It means, positively, that the various parts are interrelated and interdependent, each contributing to the welfare of the whole. Indeed, the word *system* comes from the Greek term for "standing together." Robert Worley diagrams it as the chart on the following page indicates.[10]

In Worley's diagram, the "input system" recognizes the historical and existential influence and the pooled resources of people. These enter the "transforming system" (the interior life of the church). The subsequent "output systems" refer to task forces, mission involvements, and segments of the congregation thus better equipped for life and ministry.

---

7. Ibid., p. 66.
8. Alvin J. Lindgren and Norman L. Shawchuck, *Management for Your Church: How to Realize Your Church Potential Through Systems Approach* (Nashville: Abingdon Press, 1977), pp. 26-27.
9. Ibid., p. 24.
10. Worley, *Change in the Church*, p. 78.

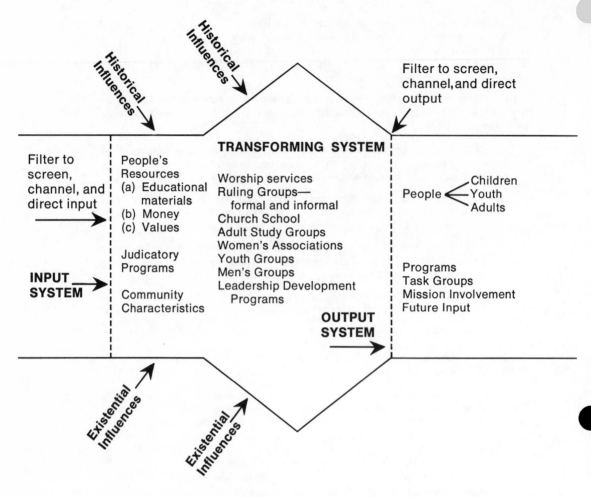

Historical Influences

Historical Influences

Historical Influences

Filter to screen, channel, and direct output

Filter to screen, channel, and direct input →

TRANSFORMING SYSTEM

People's Resources
(a) Educational materials
(b) Money
(c) Values

Judicatory Programs

INPUT SYSTEM →

Community Characteristics

Worship services
Ruling Groups—
    formal and informal
Church School
Adult Study Groups
Women's Associations
Youth Groups
Men's Groups
Leadership Development
    Programs

OUTPUT SYSTEM →

People ⟨ Children
         Youth
         Adults

Programs
Task Groups
Mission Involvement
Future Input

Existential Influences

Existential Influences

When the church is organized according to the systems theory it is closer to the biblical view than when other organizational theories are used. Because it honors both the church's "inner and outer lives," enabling it to make the fitting response to God, self, and neighbor, systems theory is especially suitable for use in the church.

Because the *systems theory* seeks to identify all the relevant components of the church and its environment, it makes possible greater effectiveness in the planning process. This is the subject of the concluding chapter.

7. The Need for Planning

Planning is the process of determining a course of action for the future. Planning, like leading, is an inclusive administrative function. Whether involved in leading, coordinating, organizing, or staffing, the administrator is simultaneously involved in planning. Though the planning function is interrelated with other administrative functions in day-to-day work, it can also be separated from them. This chapter will focus on the planning process, in order to show its linkage with the theology of the church—specifically the theology of hope.

Why plan? Why seek to determine future action? These are questions that need to be answered before discussing the planning process. We plan for theological and practical reasons.

Theologically, we plan, because we believe that God has a purpose. As Scripture indicates, his purpose can be described in various ways: He "desires all men to be saved and to come to the knowledge of the truth" (1 Tim. 2:4); "In Christ God was reconciling the world to himself, not counting their trespasses against them, and entrusting to us the message of reconciliation" (2 Cor. 5:19); "For God so loved the world that he gave his only Son, that whoever believes in him should not perish but have eternal life" (John 3:16).

God's purpose, as Scripture indicates, is redemptive. He does not function rigidly or immutably; he is, instead, set on changing the status quo, on redeeming all that exists. According to Scripture, God is purposeful.

The church is a called and commissioned people. The church exists *in* the world and for the welfare *of* the world, but it is called to carry out its mission in accordance with God's purpose *for* the world. The church is therefore God's co-worker in the world, Christ's redemptive body.

The church, as Jürgen Moltmann has stated, is future oriented.[1] Eschatology, he argues, is not a loosely attached appendix to Christian doctrine but is the basis of Christian hope, resulting in a people who are "forward looking and forward moving, and therefore revolutionizing and transforming the present." [2] Moltmann thus relates his eschatology to the changing present as if presuming a systems view of reality.

---

1. Jürgen Moltmann, *The Theology of Hope* (New York: Harper and Row, 1976).
2. Ibid., p. 16.

Linking his theology of hope to the subject of planning, he writes: "Unless hope has been aroused and is alive, there can be no stimulation for planning. Without specific goals toward which hope is directed, there can be no decision about the possibilities of planning." [3] "Planning must be aware of its origin in hope and of the projection of hope. If it puts itself in the place of hope, it loses the transcendent impetus of hope and finally also loses itself." [4] Moltmann reminds us that Christian hope has its origin in the resurrection of Christ. The cross reveals the evil of the world, its unredeemed condition. But the resurrection overpowers the evil and kindles hope anew. Therefore, people can rightly "keep their heads up, recognize meaningful goals, and find the courage to invest human and material powers with this purpose." [5] Theologically speaking, we plan because we believe God is purposeful and faithful and because we who make up the church are his agents and ambassadors in the world.

Practically, we plan because the church is a human community. Its purpose can be clarified, its goals set, and its resources allocated. Planning gives direction to the church's life. Planning focuses and releases the energies of people; it provides guidance for organizing, staffing, and programming; it integrates the work of the church. Planning, in short, enables the church to live its life and pursue its mission more responsibly.

Lou Accola lists six potential benefits to a congregation when it plans.[6]

1. Planning is a means of shaping our vision for our participation in God's mission for the church.

2. Planning helps us to reflect our convictions in ways that serve the real needs of the people.

3. Planning creates a positive, optimistic, enthusiastic mode for decision making and involvement in ministries.

4. Planning gives us a sense and expression of vision, unity, and mutual reason for being, for commitment, and for involvement.

5. Planning results in goals that give direction to the church's work and mission by focusing on desired results.

6. Planning helps us become people centered and future oriented instead of program centered and past oriented.

THE PLANNING PROCESS

While the concept of planning is motivated by both theological and practical considerations, we turn to management theory and practice for the planning process, adapting it for use in the church. The following is an outline of the steps in the planning process, with a brief description of each.

1. Formulate a mission statement

A mission statement, sometimes called a statement of purpose, identifies for the church its general mission. The statement should be inclusive enough to encompass all that the church does. Moreover, it must reflect its own "world" or context, drawing on numerous sources. The following diagram illustrates this.

---

3. Jürgen Moltmann, *Hope and Planning* (New York: Harper and Row, 1971), p. 178.
4. Ibid., p. 194.
5. Ibid., p. 198.
6. "Congregational Planning Is Not New, but the Concept Is Showing Growth," *Acts 77* (June-July 1977), Publication of The American Lutheran Church.

Here is an example of a mission statement:

> In response to the grace of God through Jesus Christ, the mission of Lutheran Church of the Good Shepherd is to affirm, interpret, and express the Christian faith through worship, education, witness, and service.

Your congregational mission statement will, of course, be tailored to your own situation.

2. Gather data

The data needed for the development of an overall plan for the church will come from two sources—the congregation itself and the community it serves. The congregation therefore conducts a *self-study*—analyzing its strengths and weaknesses; determining trends in membership, worship attendance, and stewardship; noting potential areas of need. A more sizable undertaking is the gathering of data about the community. Demographic factors, economic and political factors, and the locations and strengths of other congregations must be considered.

3. Identify needs

When the data has been gathered and interpreted, the next step is to identify the areas of need in the church and the community. What are the needs of the church for its interior life? What needs exist in the community that the congregation feasibly can serve to fulfill?

4. Set goals

Define what must happen in the interior life of the congregation if its own needs are to be met and if the congregation, in turn, is to help meet identified community needs. What must happen in worship, education, evangelism, pastoral care, stewardship? What must happen in the community? The goals when achieved will meet these needs.

A proper *goal statement* will reflect the following:
    a. It will be in harmony with the stated mission of the church.

b. It will reasonably be possible to attain.

c. It will be understandable to those working for the results it describes.

d. It will specify a target date for completion.

e. It will include cost factors, both in terms of estimated dollars and hours.

f. It will include a means of evaluation or measurement.

g. It will begin with the word *to*, followed by an active verb (never use "try to" or "encourage").

h. It will be written down.

5. Develop strategy

Here planning gets specific. A detailed strategy is worked out for allocating the resources of the congregation. This will facilitate the results that were clarified in the goal statements.

6. Implement the plan

The work of planning has been accomplished. Now the time has come to "work the plan." The respective staff, committees, and groups proceed according to plan.

7. Set time for evaluation

Systematic and ongoing review is necessary. One way to do this is to appoint a *standing evaluation committee*, which will meet regularly to monitor progress and make recommendations for needed change.

Planning is an ongoing administrative task for organizations of all kinds. The planning done by congregations, while using procedures developed by the management sciences, is motivated and guided by theological convictions. Planning results in a more responsible use of the gifts and resources God provides.

Christ makes it possible for people to be "forward looking and forward moving, therefore revolutionizing and transforming the present." In Moltmann's words, people can "keep their heads up, recognize meaningful goals, and find the courage to invest human and material powers with this purpose."

Bibliography

Adams, Arthur M. *Effective Leadership for Today's Church.* Philadelphia: The Westminster Press, 1978.

This is an excellent introduction to the entire field, theologically sound and rich in practical wisdom.

Anderson, James D. and Jones, Ezra E. *The Management of Ministry.* San Francisco: Harper and Row, 1978.

A provocative reminder that the church administration concerns not the church as an end in itself, but rather the *ministry* of the church.

Bonhoeffer, Dietrich. *Life Together.* New York: Harper and Row, 1976.

This little classic describes Bonhoeffer's experience of Christian community, a subject that deserves attention in the work of administration.

Brekke, Milo L., Strommen, Merton P., and Williams, Dorothy L. *Ten Faces of Ministry: Perspectives on Pastoral Effectiveness Based on Survey of 5000 Lutherans.* Minneapolis: Augsburg Publishing House, 1979.

This book sees administration as one of five ministry skills and spells out the type of administration people respond to most positively.

Burns, James MacGregor. *Leadership.* New York: Harper and Row, 1979.

Though written about and for the secular world, this big book has much that will help church leaders.

Drucker, Peter F. *Management: Tasks, Practices, Responsibilities.* New York: Harper and Row, 1974.

Drucker is the dean of management science. This is his landmark work, over 800 pages.

Engstrom, Ted W. and Dayton, Edward R. *Strategy for Leadership.* Old Tappan, New Jersey: Fleming H. Revell Co., 1979.

This book provides a clear application of management insights for Christian organizations. Strong on management by objectives.

Feucht, Oscar E. *Everyone a Minister.* St. Louis: Concordia Publishing House, 1974.

An interesting and provocative expression of the priesthood of all believers, with practical applications to today's church.

Greenleaf, Robert K. *Servant Leadership: A Journey into the Nature of Legitimate Power and Greatness.* New York: Paulist Press, 1977.

Greenleaf first develops the "servant-leader" concept and then applies it to institutions as well as to various kinds of leaders.

Hersey, Paul and Blanchard, Kenneth H. *Management of Organizational Behavior: Utilizing Human Resources,* 3rd ed. Englewood Cliffs: Prentice-Hall, 1977.

A helpful source from the secular world that focuses on the behavioral approach to organizational life.

Hutcheson, Richard G. Jr. *Wheel Within the Wheel.* Atlanta: John Knox Press, 1979.

This is one of the best attempts to bridge the gap between management science and theology. Balanced and thorough.

Keating, Charles J. *The Leadership Book.* New York: Paulist Press, 1978.

This good little book relates insights from the behavioral sciences to the life of the church. A good place to begin.

Moltmann, Jürgen. *Hope and Planning.* New York: Harper and Row, 1971.

An application of the theology of hope to the work of planning in a Christian organization.

Niebuhr, H. Richard. *The Purpose of the Church and Its Ministry.* New York: Harper and Row, 1977.

From this study of the aims of theological education, Niebuhr clarifies his "pastoral director" image of the parish minister.

Parish Planning Resource. Minneapolis: Augsburg Publishing House, 1978.

This is a valuable and practical resource for planning in the church. It provides good rationale and step-by-step suggestions for procedure.

Rudge, Peter F. *Ministry and Management.* Scranton: Barnes and Noble, 1968.

A thorough exploration into organizational theory, which, in turn, is linked to doctrinal analogies. Provocative.

Worley, Robert C. *Change in the Church: A Source of Hope.* Philadelphia: The Westminster Press, 1971.

Worley explores the need for organizational structures and leadership styles that are most appropriate for the church.